The Master Letters

The Master Letters

POEMS BY

Lucie Brock-Broido

ALFRED A. KNOPF   NEW YORK

2013

THIS IS A BORZOI BOOK
PUBLISHED BY ALFRED A. KNOPF, INC.

The author wishes to thank editors of journals in which versions of poems have appeared:

THE AGNI REVIEW: *I Dont Know Who It Is That Sings, nor Did I, Would I Tell; You Can't Always Get What You Want; Everybody Has a Heart, Except Some People; The Interrupted Life; His Apprentice; A Brief History of Asylum*

ANTAEUS: *Evangelical*

THE AMERICAN POETRY REVIEW: *The Last Passenger Pigeon in the Cincinnati Zoo; Bodhisattva; When the Gods Go, Half-Gods Arrive; Carnivorous; Her Habit; Obsession, Compulsion; Work*

BOULEVARD: *Prescient*

THE COLORADO REVIEW: *Treason*

DENVER QUARTERLY: *Housekeeping; Also, None Among Us Has Seen God; Desunt Non Nulla; And You Know That I Know Milord That You Know; The October Horse; Everything Husk to the Will; Fair Copy from a Fair World; Rampion; Gratitude; A Glooming Peace This Morning with It Brings*

HARVARD MAGAZINE: *Pursuit of Happiness*

THE HARVARD REVIEW: *Rome Beauty; In the Attitude Desired for Exhibition; Radiating Naïveté; Am Moor; Grimoire; Did Not Come Back*

INDIANA REVIEW: *Dull Weather; Toxic Gumbo; Pompeian*

THE KENYON REVIEW: *From the Proscenium; Unholy*

THE NEW YORKER: *Carrowmore*

THE PARIS REVIEW: *Haute Couture Vulgarity; Into Those Great Countries of the Blue Sky of Which We Don't Know Anything; And Wylde for to Hold; How Can It Be I Am No Longer I*

PARNASSUS: POETRY IN REVIEW: *Your Cromwell, Your Thomas More; For the Lustrum; Like Murder for Small Hay in the Underworld; Moving On in the Dark Like Loaded Boats at Night, Though There Is No Course, There Is Boundlessness; To a Strange Fashion of Forsaking; The Sleeping Hollow of His Face Will Be the Straight Pass of Surrendering*

PLOUGHSHARES: *The Supernatural Is Only the Natural, Disclosed*

VERSE: *That Same Vagabond Sweetness; At the River Unshin's Edge*

Earlier versions of *A Preamble to The Master Letters* appeared in THE KENYON REVIEW and in THE AMERICAN POETRY REVIEW.

Emily Dickinson MS 828 used by permission of Amherst College Library, Special Collections, and by the Houghton Library, Harvard University. Reprinted by permission of the publishers from *The Letters of Emily Dickinson*, edited by Thomas H. Johnson, Cambridge, Massachusetts: The Belknap Press of Harvard University Press, copyright © 1958, 1986 by the President and Fellows of Harvard College.

Library of Congress Cataloging-in-Publication Data

Brock-Broido, Lucie.
    The master letters: poems/by Lucie Brock-Broido.—1st ed.
        p.   cm.
    ISBN 0–679–44174–3 (hc.); ISBN 0–679–76599–9 (pbk.)
    I. Title.
PS3552.R6145M37   1995   95–30284
811'.54—dc20   CIP

Published October 17, 1995
First Paperback Edition Published April 4, 1997
Third Printing, January 2005

FOR MY MOTHER
VIRGINIA GREENWALD

Master:

If you saw a bullet
hit a Bird and he told you
he wasn't shot, you might
at his Courtesy but you would
certainly doubt his word.
One drop more from the
bottle stains your Lady's
bosom — then would you
Thomas' faith his Anatomy
stronger than his faith in you.
God made me — ~~master~~ I did
not — myself. Hurt — knew
it was done — He built the
heart in me — By and by
it outgrew me — And like
the little Mother — with the
big Child — I got tired
holding him — I heard of a
thing called Redemption — quiet
the men and women —

A Preamble to *The Master Letters*

I

Emily Dickinson left, along with her fascicles of poems, three documents known as the Master Letters. In the week following Dickinson's death in May of 1886, her sister Lavinia found these in a locked box containing hundreds of poems. Even though these missives were penned as elaborate drafts suitable for mailing (the final letter, for instance, was composed on laid paper, cream with a blue rule, & embossed with a queen's head above the letter L)—there is doubt whether fair copies were ever posted or even if they were ever designed to be posted. The identity of the intended recipient remains unknown.

Two of these letters begin with the vocative—*Dear Master*. The third is to a Recipient Unknown. The letters may have been written to Samuel Bowles, or to the Reverend Charles Wadsworth. Or they may have been to a lover, or to God.

These are gracious, sometimes nearly erotic, worshipful documents, full of Dickinson's dramas of entreaty & intimacy, her distances—the Queen Recluse, little girl, the mystic, the breathless renouncer. *The Wife—without the Sign! Betrothed—without the swoon.* Dickinson, a master fabricator herself, imagined or addressed her Master in earnest, & the letters, like many of her love poems, are unabashed & urgent "bulletins from Immortality."

Dickinson, in all her surviving correspondence, was not known to have invented *letters* as fictive documents. Yet these three missives maintain the lyric density, the celestial stir, her high-pitched cadences, her odd Unfathomable systems of capitalization, the peculiar swooning syntax, the fluid stutter of her verse.

II

The following fifty-two poems, a series of latter-day Master Letters, echo formal & rhetorical devices from Dickinson's work. The first three, originally conceived as prose, were intended as a specific & finite homage to Dickinson's triptych—her *brocade devastations*. But my original impulse—the epistle procession (that impure, irresistible form of prose which lies on top of poetry)—gave way to an Other, coupled, more sinewy form. The third form fashioned was sterner still, the Old World sonnet—but American & cracked, *the odd marriage between hysteria & haiku.*

A Preamble to The Master Letters

III

On the fabrication of the Master: he began as a Fixed star. He was particular. Over a period of a year, then another, then more years, my idea of the Master began an uprush—he became a kind of vortex of tempests & temperaments, visages & voicelessness. He took on the fractured countenance of a composite portrait, police-artist sketch. Editor, mentor, my aloof proportion, the father, the critic, beloved, the wizard—he was beside himself.

On the Speaker: at first, she was a brood of voice—a flock of women with Dickinson as mistress of the skein, the spinning wheel, the Queen Domestic, composed and composing, as she did, from her looms & room & seclusion. *Remoteness is the founder of sweetness.* Raids on other work began— Sappho, Bradstreet, Brontë, Akhmatova, Plath. *When I state Myself, as representative of the Verse—it does not mean me—but a Supposed Person.* Then, a lustrum into the composition, I signed a poem—L.

On the fabrication of the poem (Ezra Pound on Robert Frost): *Definition of Prayer—Dear Lord, pay attention to*—me.

IV

In the early summer of 1883, Dickinson wrote—*Dear Friend—You are like God. We pray to Him, & He answers "No." Then we pray to Him to rescind the "No," & He don't answer at all* . . .

Contents

Contents

(O N E)

Notes on some of the poems follow the text on page 78

Carrowmore

All about Carrowmore the lambs
Were blotched blue, belonging.

They were waiting for carnage or
Snuff. This is why they are born

To begin with, to end.
Ruminants do not frighten

At anything—gorge in the soil, butcher
Noise, the mere graze of predators.

All about Carrowmore
The rain quells for three days.

I remember how cold I was, the botched
Job of travelling. And just so.

Wherever I went I came with me.
She buried her bone barrette

In the ground's woolly shaft.
A tear of her hair, an old gift

To the burnt other who went
First. My thick braid, my ornament—

My belonging I
Remember how cold I will be.

Also, None Among Us Has Seen God

My Most Courteous Lord—

The Teutons have their word for keeping Quiet which our blessing
Language does not have. To say nothing of—*Agone*, to say nothing

Of the monk who set himself ablaze, in autumn hair & all, the ravish
& the wool of him, the mourning & the sweetest smell of him—Alive—

How did you teach the learning of this Holding & the holding
Back—To say nothing of—*Ago*, obedience, the hiding in

The feral peace of speaking Not, the root & oath of it—
Old as a prehistoric furrow horse abed in awe & sediment,

Curled on his runic side, in the shape of an O, broken. Wake
Is agape, an outskirt of agony, blouse-white & bad—To say

Nothing of the nook of sleep—which is a ravage in the chamois night-
Sweat of your raff & shames, the fevers of a minor fire, the rage

Or punishment, the *Agapé*, the kerosene & bone-red rag.
That was the best moment of his life. The burning down.

Rome Beauty

My mother says in the beautiful
Rome Beauty of my wild head—

She wishes to decore the one bad
Spot, the mottled mishap in the road,

Fawn accident, the one dun
Bruise & just that one

& I'll be beauty, whole—where all the demons
Dine collectively on game, the momentous dumb

Switching of the great silvery utensils carrying on
In the gentry's red lit looming dining halls

Like cervine tails twitching in bad weather—*Heaven
Paints its wild irregularity*—When hunger dulls

The peasants harvesting the lesion's fall, I will
Be beautiful, gazelle.

Unholy

Dear Master—

Last night I slept in Mutiny, woke surrounded by the scent of citrus, just as day dilated like an eye peering telescopically over a rough sea of Sentimentia, spying an island after weeks on weeks of nothing but navy, an occasional predatory sea-bird, a gratuitous cloud, no noise except water & then after that more water—& spied land. When I was young I sold slow French kisses as dry goods to sailors—as some girls made madmoney in more genteel ways, I had none of this.

It is unfortunate, especially in this hour of the millennium, to seek the Captain's calloused hand. He is more accustomed to handling rope, rough-whiskered sturdy twines, the perseverance of the sail as it ascends its mast & bursts like a god into the nautical knots of ruffian wind. He is so less used to handling the religious limbs of women, their finer slender arms, unbaptized clavicles, spleening, the Hopefull countenance.

As I explained, there is no Harm in Contrivances; there is little left to speak of save the long Unarcking Moment of post-coital estrangement, the untwined two blinking into the raw mottled air of a dim bedroom, uncoiling like that, windless, little left to say in a Terminal Voyaging. Let us say, for instance, there are but six things left to feel in the world, six things left to put your mouth on: *Bliss & Loss*—for two, *Trembling & Compulsion*—four, *Desire & Disease*—you see? Gerbil! Noodle! Little One.

Do not think me, Sir, distended with self-pity; far from my own lean truth. It's this devil of the ventriloquist bending my lackey's back again. My voice thrown, my Other littler self on my own knee, practicing a sleight of hand, the tongue of the Inventor wagging the tongue of the Invented. It is true that each self keeps a secret self which cannot speak when spoken to.

Parts of the mouth are not clean, unholy by growing old I am afraid. In the funneled obsequious rooms of each house, the sails go slack—to nowhere; it is spring & nothing hurts so much as—*this.*

Unholy

When I was sixteen & played Miss Julie for a year, he said: *Take the broom*. And I took the broom. And he said: *Sweep*. And I swept.

From the Scurvy City,
very earnestly—

Your Scholar

A Brief History of Asylum

My innocence diminishes in the thrall
Of a New World symmetry, a burial

Grounded in the anatomies of Virginia's earth—
The wetlands filling in & shifting common

Wealth with soil, sprung markers steep
Above the fallen alder leaves, askewed.

Did not the eyes of Lunatics look
Differently? Somehow asymmetrical—

The white girl's odd black iris
Narrow, pupils belladonnaed wide, high

As a bird of prey crossing
The sky's staired plain.

I am angel, addict, catherine wheel—a piece of work
On fire spinning sparks from Lourdes to Alexandria.

I press my face against the Aprilled rainy glass,
Rose at the throat, rose at the windless

Porthole, radiant mullion at the wheel window's wheel.
The hunters pursuing & the hounds pursuing—

& I a Jew in a hoot-owl's rood loft—
Innocence diminishing at the speed of

A baying foxhound wild for hunger or for love.
In the troop, savanna, clan of invalid or swamp,

A hood of souls gone maundering, moonstruck
& medieval in the tower's eternal Method of things.

And the night cold & the night long & the river
To cross—trepanning the fissure—caves of the Wish.

A Brief History of Asylum

At a century's torsion, they began the trespass
Of the cranium—lobation, incision, wheelworks

Stilled & listening—House of Some Lords. From
The skull's bony porthole, rivers unbound & ran

Out—mandate of docile, mandate of Sweet, no roaring
Subaltern pain. The temples—yielding, lamblike, mild—

Invalid to sorrow—right half, left half, limbic & all
For memory or love—I am subject, subjugate, inthralled.

The Supernatural Is Only
the Natural, Disclosed

At your feet, I am a shoemaker's apprentice,
Toxic in a long day of fumes. I'm listening

To the fluorescent light come on
In April, flinging a hot white scarf

Across a month mottled by the chemicals
Of eastern standard time, in the spokes of wheels

Of hormones turning in an unseasoned sky. In a gospel
According to Hunters, you name your bird

Without a gun. You sit & watch as one does in the woods,
Contemplating prey, awefully. You have a heart

As large as a silver cleat, small thing.
I should have liked to see you, before you became improbable.

In your woods, I would not name the flowers—
They bother me, spicy & devout as they are, perennial & full

Of the pretense of sweetness & decline.
You dazzle me.

In the wilderness, the blacksmiths & the cobblers leave
Their machinery on all night, greased

By the nasty oils of midnight
Till the custodian slips off the switch at dawn.

Should you, before this reaches you, experience Immortality,
Who will inform me of the exchange?

I entreat you—Sir—in your next white wove
Missive to call my name—correctly—just

This once. The continual misspelling
Is a form of sorcery, it smacks

Of heresy. It would bereave—
Your Gnome

Obsession, Compulsion

The Breath is as much of Mob as I can master, love. Steamy
It comes on the winter's windowglass in the shapes of the faces

Of philosophers, there Aristotle's white crown & brow blown
Like the etching of a hunting dog covering tracks in the snow

With his paws. I felt a quiver like the quarry giving in. I'm a drop
In a thimble of boys to you Sir. I am glad to be born, ungroomed.

Did I displease you—But wont you tell me how?
The hounds, let loose from the iron gate, surrender their miles

Of packed marks in the snow travelling—away from home
They follow my life like a fence through the yards of rush

Grass where larger, muter animals than they stand—hooves
On the ground's hearth—& bear it, standing still. I stay indoors,

The heart's clean home; a thought is fire's phantom snuffed
Last night. Obsession helps me up the stairs at night, past

My Father's door—I watched his breath go clear & thin then flicker
Out, in Indian summer near noon one day. Thank you for your

Affections, even Veiled; I am compelled to travel to my bed
Each night alone in down, scoured as a holystone, the hounds gathered

At the gate outside, staining the snow with their treasure,
Their kill. By morning I will comb & curry them.

I will remember you forgetting & bear this, lying—down—

> *Would you but guide, your—*
> Punitive Divine

When the Gods Go, Half-Gods Arrive

If it is true that you were young
Once, a demiurge & did

This—tell me then, supernatural
One, exactly how

Many days I have left to wake into
& witness the things

Of this world holding on,
The hunched pillbug holding onto

Its hump of hill, witness the boy
In radiation walking straight-

Faced into a radiant room which will burn him
Just to stay here, be—alive—how many nights.

How much will I be changed, before I
Am changed?

I've missed
A good deal of pageantry by being born

A Jew, the Christian paramour's a thing
Of tensile strength, all cling

& desperation. Or was it boys then
When you longed to run

Your hands along the plumes
Of muscle, limb, Amish

In their austerity of flesh.
In my dominion, to die is to turn

Completely, gorged
With change, bound

To a Jew's shoeless no life
After this one is.

When the Gods Go, Half-Gods Arrive

Once, you knew the powers
Of conversion, white powder cut

With nothing on the scales,
Delicate, Pythagorean, bold as a compass

Needle pointing—North, a commerce
Of tiny clean white envelopes,

Your letters to me long since
Lost, I've been loving you so long.

And Wylde for to Hold

On the chine of the first white inkling of the winter
The Ravenmaster wraps his limbs in combs of wind.

It is November; the tower closes down
For night. He is wont to dwell on

Bridles, stars, medieval presaging. I will be ringed
At ankle, am a corvid thing.

Ruin is formal.
Metal, tether, one good name.

Virgin wool still with the body's
Oils keeps the cold, an augury.

A man who lives in a circular
Stair keeps watch.

The lighthouse I let go of, as a girl.
Since in your hand you seek to tame

Me, ravening, am wont to salt my own—
My will be done.

He breeds the bird to clip its wings.
Form is mortal & habitual.

As for my own limbs which are flightless
As a fortress knuckled to the earth,

As for my Own—I am hewn.
Ask others, whether I do lie.

Lack of water, lack of light,
Lack of heat, lack of bedding, I should go

On this way forever; it is my wont to go.
Tonight—the wind will be high in its scaffolding,

On the strength. I will listen for its habit
Especially about the throat like an Elizabethan cuff

And Wylde for to Hold

At the crude nest of the mouth. Our bed
Will be lined with shredded bark from sycamore & hair.

Let them lie broad awake in their nest, scissoring.
None will fly.

As for my own—I will line my speech
Like the seven mottled & pale

Eggs, incubating, after being held Round
So long. None will fly.

And wild to hold,
And wild to shame,

And wild to wreathe,
And wild to tame.

At the River Unshin's Edge

The granite steps do not stop for the water's
Bank, but enter it & I don't know

If the castle's composer meant such
Suicide, or if the land has just gone under

Viscous waters in six centuries.
From Lough Arrow, the waters leak north

Till the clear distinctions between swamp
Or lake or river blur;

My white dress will
Be leaded down with juniper

& sinew, brink. *The blood*—after all—
Is more showy than the Breath.

At the River Unshin's edge
The species are prolific, even this

Far north—the cypress trees, the eucalyptus
Bough, the hemlock's homicidal spell, a cast

& prong, malignancy.
Everything begets here & you

Would walk the six steps into
It with me. Silique of mustards, briar, wrack,

Long after in the reeds of the long aftergrass.
A bastard schooner transgresses

The angelica, feverroot blisters, the hyssop
Flowers going on & on. The fireboat

Will slip its slip into the water's grave
Soliloquy. I will be drunk on it

At the River Unshin's Edge

Tonight, an invitation of the thicket
Of one composer's bloodless dread.

The dying is more gaudy than
The death you know.

Carnivorous

I was lying loose from God. Strange is it not best
Beloved, in the New World, in this skinny life,

Intemperate with chance, my spirit quickens
For the fall's estate. In India, the half

Hour is the hour, we were like that then—
Jammed wrong & wrong in the diurnal

Mangy chambers of our carnall
Hearts, the rose robes rustling loose as velvet

Curtains at the stage prow, passing
Into the strange salt air of an Indian

Ocean, hoarding kindling, heading
West with hours, later than we might

Have known, counting tins of meats & oil left,
If they should lose or last the night.

To a Strange Fashion of Forsaking

late winter

Master—

I hardly know to address you; you are—a man? Anon to dust. *Warum bin ich ich, und nicht du?*

Loved—I think I may never have touched your linen, nor your skin. It is winter again. What with crimped winds & a small Berlin of snow, I think it will be always this one way. Soon, I will be travelling by train—through it. I am seized with a small fever now; I cannot get small enough.

We were all vaccinated the other day. Some of the others dreamt of cows, or lambs at best. I write to you from an hour of broad linguistic flux— dialects of north & south mingling, the iodine of the east diminishing, leaving its rust stain to the voice. In the frozen ground, the earth apples lie like unborn calves; you are older than you used to be.

I want to know two things by the next person who writes:
Tell me—*When,*   & then—*How will it happen?*

I renounce Nothing. I am imprinted erotically with—One. I will need the scarf about my mouth to quiet me. I am overheated by hard riding. Dartmoor prison is a beautiful place to be punished in. So thick the deciduous rash of the woods—contagious as a small pox in a small city quartered— the language abandons rapidly to form new strains, resistant, unbridled like that, & not surrendering.

Forsaking all others—anon to dust, I will not marry. *Though I myself be bridled of my mind.* Horizontal, without sentiment, in a bed of clematis & not say nay. Storm excites me, *Schadenfreude.* Even anonymity. I have no daughter—now. My father died two times. I am an extraordinary I & not you. Is this what you may call suffering?

That is my charge—

Did Not Come Back

In the roan hour between then & then again, the now, in the Babel
Of a sorrel ship gone horizontal to a prow of night, the breach of owls

Abducted by broad light, but blind, in the crime, the titanesque of rare
Assault—we who have come back—petitioning, from the chair

Electric with bad news, from the stunning, from the narrows
Of an evening gall, from the mooring of an hour slanted on the follow

Bow, she rose from a bed of Ireland like a flyted trout, a shiny
Marvel on the sailor's deck, an apologia—divining—

As once, as at a salted empire port, he washed
Her fleeted body & they lied, the best of them, the cream & crush

Of this, the madrigal & sacrifice of that, the best of them,
The slowest velvet suffocation of their kind, did not come

Whittled back by autumn, at an hour between thorn & chaff,
Not come riddled with oblivion, the crossing & a shepherd's staff,

The moment between Have & Shall Not Want, we who have salt
Always know, that we who have—the best of us—did not come back.

(TWO)

And You Know That I Know
Milord That You Know

That I had no idea I had been travelling
In the scrying light, crutched friar roaming

Snow-apple orchards every autumn,
Clutching the fireless stricken lantern

Of your feudal dark. It was not known
To me to stop there in the scarce

Field of the cold country, constant, Prussian,
Quickened & set the shunt lamp down:

The exquisite extinguishing,
The adumbrated thing.

In the monarchy of me, my ritual
& tinctured mouth, I had no idea that I

Had wandered like a torch-monk cowled
In the dulcet life—Deceive & now

Be done with it. Each night, you loose
Your face in the dauntless, dusted temple

Of my hair. Each fall, relentless, willingly—
You were numberless & kill the light.

The October Horse

I

Shepherd—Fasten him to the hearth
Of the house, the right-hand horse.

Old Autumn, same rude ritual—hung on
The fir-tree on the last October night.

Old Autumn, rough horse muscle—Done
By us. *I had a yearning I could tell to none.*

I have been trying, since the autumn's
Wield, to practice a simplicity.

Coppers, brasses, rite encumbers me.
I am surrounded by the metals

Of the implements—steam
Of engines—long esophagi

Of trains, the coach inconstant,
Rough, the landscape immaterial.

I have been artless, since September,
To habit a rusticity. All my oddments need

Be carriaged by a hired hand.
I possess too many things,

Cannot be quit—acquiring.
Beside the river, corn will ripen

In the new rude moon. Sickle on
The crown lands, travelling.

Gourds will plump & wither
On the vine if unattended to.

Needs must gather the Kinds
Of grain—then thrash & winnow it.

I I

Here, in the north, the horse
Stands still. Machine keeps

Its swallow in the dark.
The plough ox carries on his work.

Shadows ripen at the clock
By line by line by line.

Dwarf star stands still, hindered
By the things of me, his brief

Arms full of me, of injury.
The train keeps cutting the corridor

In weather against it, or
Neither Here nor there.

I've not a sinew of nonchalance in me.
I miss the weight of him above me,

Me on him, hands empty for an hour
Clenched, the brood of ritual.

Old autumn, shepherd, right-
Hand horse—with host

Or yet alone, in heaven or at hearth—
Some how or no how, I propose, Sir, to see you.

Her Habit

Master—

Because I was in the habit of you & because I have an ardor for the lie, *I cannot speak until I know.*

I have watched for you up & down the long clay path, demi-daily. Sometimes I think I hear you in the solemn bark of birds, or the cantering of dogs as they bring home their quarry—gently—in their mouths, no pierced skin, no feathers askew, only the unbruised slant of a neck broken by fear, limp now & perfect in the fluidity of damaged Form.

Have I told you I have quit taking any meats whatsoever? A mortal signal, a deference to form, it is to me a form of Prayer. *I got a bad whim.*

In truth, I have innumerable habits; I was a-Bed today. My world is as ordered as if—as if I had stacked the stars in the nightsky's orchard, senseless as crates of fish stacked glimmering, one-eyed & blank, one atop the other of them, cold as Rome apples or a new moon.

To all except great dread, the heart adjusts.

I do not let go it, because it is—
Mine

Prescient

Master—you were having your veins cleaned out of Me—
A burred spike down the artery's shaft, thistling.

You have the catchweed of quiet on your tongue, I have
The power of speech. Parts of the body will always live

By the lair—by November the pine boughs will corrugate my
Yard. A shock of Needles shook loose from their limb & I live

In a burgeon of nettles, in an emergency of old leaves from
The absurd magnolia which grew so hard to bloom

Twice this year & Failed, sterile
As a divination based on wish & wish & wish.

Forecast—Nothing ever felt like This.
Forecast—Hound Dog.

Forecast—The Incidents may presage war.
Forecast—I am my love—*a Lucky girl.*

Gratitude

I am alive, this morning—
& am alive—numbed

By field gray halcion, dulled by the gift
Of boiling water, the freedom to descend

My own glassed stairs, to wind
The century clock, to know

I am old enough to know—a long time Ago.
I remember Everything, remember everything.

From me—Sir—you have memorized my gift
For blister & audacity. From you—a gift

Only of a mute, the null of the janitor
Sweeping alone at night with his orange

Push broom in the fallout shelter.
It is—*Only—Motion, & am dumb.*

Dull Weather

Rises, sets, by my own hand, dog days end.
Even my self reminds me of you.

I cannot refrain from Ruin.
You coach your boys to violence, even in peculiar

Heat. They are hairless, clean as copper
Coins made new in a New England mint, doomed

To be spent. Your form is
Neanderthal in its simplicity—simplicity is

Bliss. *This is the world that opens,*
Shuts, flutters like the lashed Eye

Of a porcelain doll set down in its humpbacked
Trunk—by September you were only Sleeping,

Only—Cooler, frost, in dull
Weather plough, do not fail me now.

From the Proscenium

early January

My Dear Sir—

The year thus far has gone Blank. True, it is a new one, but it is too cold thus far for any Weather to take hold. The high winds blow the pilots out at night & sometimes I have gone shimmering into ungentle sleep. I know you like to hear about my seasons here; it is one thing we can speak of equally. (

Regarding my Tudor Disregard for the words which bleed out on me in ink—exhale & listen closely to me now or cut me loose. All gods secretly wish to be women—baroque, fecund, vulgar, sweet. It's an old script I read aloud & the theatre is empty tonight.

I play for the Balconies, all velvet-backed maroon chairs, slightly hyperbolic like a coast guard sailor calling out to fog through a primitive megaphone, looking out for One left by the wreck, still clinging to a cleaving rock. Rouged in the face so the facial features can be seen in storm.

How can something this Small take up such space? A Soul enters & a room fills with an odd light as if a lung took in the first Homely glint coming from the wreck of an Elizabethan cargo ship—till my heart is so Full as pure sail, I cannot breathe.

In the Heights this evening, the Grief Group collects in the basement of a bad girls' School. Charity, Hope. Not penitentiary, but more of a blind girls' home, basement of brooms & broom-makers where no one ever gets out with Sight.

Infinity is true. And that which cannot be Taken back goes on like a Sixth Act, washing over & over a tutored undercurrent off the coast, which circles, which gives in, repeating itself iambically like the pulse of every thing which goes on beating—

Into the loams of night, like meat veins in a white urn, fashioned after the Greek, in the old style of the Old World.

From the Proscenium

In the rash of scarlet fever, in your scarlet dreams, all the stakes were high
& the theatre filled with donors urgent to contribute to your cause. You
kicked the covers off, febrile, aching in the thighs, uncovered your covers
for many nights in the proscenium of your bed, until the fever broke & the
chase stopped & the Weather entered the room to cool you, to come back
to me.

A chorus on stilts, all of us long-legged girls chanting that way we do, all
syncopation, all Grief. This scarlatina line. Would you remember me after
a scant season of forgetting, the noise of amnesia when memory is an or-
chestra in its pit, lost on the page? The woodwinds gone wrong. The
second violinist gone mad. The harp player Fallen, forefingers poised on
the sheepgut strings, all bewildered, the pages disordered—into the disson-
ant Faith of a song transcribed in the wrong incantation?

Faith to you Sir; the bad girls weave by rote—even if they cannot see.
Grace to you Sir. Hand for the Wife.

> Blue hat to the Sailors, who never give in.
> I am—
>
> *Your,*
> *Faithfull Friend*

Radiating Naïveté

I am a false philosopher of this
World, a steady congregation

Of one, nobody's panther, nobody's
Tinny cigarbox, nobody's violin, no

Midsummer naïf in Havana rain.
I am glad to see the summer dying

Off, the umbrage of the cornfields, breast-
High stalks gone brittle in the drought.

The headlights early coming on, dusk
Is an old adjective, color of the blind

Reading their prayer in pocks.
You should have been

A contender, a Canadian dime mixed
Up in our own, worthless & shiny, jamming

Up vending machines & roadside phones,
Old Indian. The harvest will

Be small this year & dear—
I'm nobody's truck farmer, nobody's juke,

Nobody's cold sweat on the wooden front porch,
Nobody's southern heartbreak hill.

I'm wide-eyed as Louis Armstrong when he woke
Moonlit in his darkened motel room: all

My white soprano injuries.
I am acquisitive, I pray

Alone. In the ashes, nobody's isotope,
No glass of milk. Nobody's stained-

Radiating Naïveté

Glass messages, not the radium
In its dish, wide-eyed

As Madame Curie, lit
By half-lives at her hand,

Nobody's sin, nobody's white-
Knuckled god, nobody's humming bird.

Bodhisattva

I was cowering at the circumference
Of your heart, howling when you weren't

Looking East at me, religiously.
I have minuscule Hindu thoughts & wide

Ideas like Muddy Waters many-handed
In a Chicago pub, north

Of Nirvana, singing out
His soul's lungs, born like a baby with no

Milkteeth, no Word, no leg left to stand on.
When the murderer went to his electric

End, at dawn, the citizens lined in that odd
Blue morning light like birds

Of paradise congregated on a wire, picketing the stay
Of execution—*Have a Seat*—they said & he did.

There was this wood-note down
The Mississippi Valley where I live

In a world of just
& equal punishments, some blues, an eye

For eyes, you
Awaken, bodhisattva, come

Back home to me, I gather
You in all my many arms & run my fingers

Through your silver hair,
Prehensile as a primate's deepest fear

Of falling from the great grey greave
Of limb, to the ground, where the gatherers

Gather what berries
Are left, this time of year.

Fair Copy from a Fair World

Master, my tinsmith—

Then there is quiet. Light scars like the foxed pages of an old germanic text; you mottle at the touch. *The light goes out a first time.*

The century—an implement polished by the scythesmiths; seasons heaving; hours blinding in a heaven of perpetual laboring.

When I woke stitched in the cicatrix of our fair drab bed, I was mute. A voice bound by the long worn muslin of a mortal work. I would want to marry now, as Thomas said again, the Absences. *I didn't be—myself.*

In the economy of a tinker's cult, the goldsmiths structure all their tools alchemically. There, they fashion needles out of base & metalled cold. There, where they invoke the silver eye, transparent thread threads through, one fisheye wanders like the fox light on the hard floor of the Friar's room.

At five they loose the coppery churchbells on the parish here. Sky the color of a seam of swallows rushing on this old New World. Color of thrush, color of thrush. Then, there is quiet.

Everyone is asleep, light metals, mender wandering. Needle, thread—were precious there.

Two ravens, travelling at night most times, in flocks, collect in the blacksmith's oak by dusk, their feet fastened to the branch bowed by their tinny weight, perfectly, like a fair copy of a document Done. I was facile, as you know.

Your Aff—
Scholar

His Apprentice

You did not state your price. When you took
On the post of schoolmaster on the final day

Of Lent, you punished your own. In that age darkness
Came on early, over the fields of bunch

Grass, wire, English rye, the brass bells
Of the high church chiming every hour, hallowing

You home for supper; when the young boys turned
Clockwise in their straw beds & covered

Themselves with wools & wheat, you came home
Before a sallow harvest to recite your Latin

Prayers in bed at night. This is when I dreamed
You centuries ago, on my knees when I slid

Your high black boots off & laid
Them side by side at the foot

Of my bed, when you wanted me as much
As promises & fame, the necromances

With the long gone, those who rose
Out of their stopped steps to come

Blink at you in the fire's leathered
Eye, when you harrowed the lines of the backs

Of the bones of my hand, the gold
Bunch of my hair, the alchemy of my merely

Mortal form, unspoilt yet
By stars, physicians, aristocracy.

You Can't Always Get What You Want

eve of November

Sir,

Light of your loins—I have been to the ruins & come back with art. All season, the pigeons have found their way indoors somehow, trapped in the cellar, soiling the floors & the walls with their exterminating terrors, blind as babies upside down.

I know you have suffered, Sir. Since September I have seen a buck pinned against the chrome elaborate grating of a German Daimler as it moves across America in the middle of a century. Of violence, my love, two nights ago the city of Detroit went up in flames, women's faces on the news railroaded by weeping, bloody town, a devilish night of bonding, the sharing of blood Promises. *All boys should be nicer.*

All blazing autumnal melancholia converges with the end of daylight saving time. A rain storm all night long—all carnage, all wind, all hallows. Soon the tubercular dusk will enter my chamber like a bloodcolored candle snuffing out, this early in the afternoon. There are no sorcerers left, only mechanics to fix things as they break down.

You get what you need. I am invited, with religious frequency in parking lots, to be Saved, to convene, to partake in redemptive ritual, to come back to the small circle of prayers. I go on, alone, ever aware of the great algebraic equations which keep this world aloft. The stuff which sets the neons wild at night. The dolls are rocked in their woven baskets, the demimonde of the nursery.

No baby yet. Starlings cross the highways in shapes of colossal ruins crumbling down. How long is an hour in an afterlife. Tea on a silver service, the girlchild servant devoted, doting on—

>		*the amenities of dusk, the aristocracy*
>		*of servitude, how long she has been in*
>		*the orchard watching the light transfusions*
>		*as the night quicksilvers—intravenously—*
>		*a blooding opened from its vein to Air.*

Pursuit of Happiness

August

Revd Sir—

I really am sorry that you are falln out with the Spiritual World, especially if I should have to answer for it.

There were so many nights I sat on the wooden stairs of my porch & listened to the biremes of the crickets' wings rowing & rowing deep into the darkness. Down the long coffin of the Mississippi.

A Wilderness Lord.

As if the moon would be Full as a brain not right this Dark—which is true—wherever you are, a hollow legend or blue willow plate. Or wherever you have been. *I pray you—*

Will to meet me in the orchard's shagged or shadowed southern light, the low rub of cicadas indexing their oil & eventide, then I would tell you—everything.

I send a message by a Mouth that cannot speak.

(T H R E E)

A Glooming Peace This Morning with It Brings

The sedative of frost composes
Its infinity of dormant melodramas

On the glass. It consoles one,
The solstice of the hour's no

Apparent motion, standing still.
It contents one, the solace of

Form & phantasm, of sieve
& specter, root & disposition.

The difference between desire & compulsion
Is that one is wanting, one is warding off.

Consort—submission is a form of brawling
Of the hearts, & one is Sped—a stroke or flaw

Inflicted northward, southward, pardoned still.
A plague on both our wills.

Housekeeping

After the Zhivago of it all, the terrible sleeve
Of ice, cataracted, relentless am I now to weave

You through a season of small thaw, am I to hire
The grappling hooks to fish the winter's

Missing implements from the river's whipstitched
Seams, my self a beckoned pharos as I light the switch

In your corridor of kitchen dark. You have been outside
The body now. And the sled cuts the snow one half

A world away, here—burden beasts are dead of it.
The hoary load, metalled spoons on leather strops, the cleft

Of blade—forgive me for how long it takes to mend
The tear in the body's tailored skin

Like the Siberian boy in autopsy
Stitched shut at last, & asymmetrically.

Rampion

I know the pathos & the Peculiar & the cramped soul. I know the orchard, the ungoverned, the bunched & sightless hive, the quince & crockery. I know the sudden light of snow, bundling, like a field of rampion run wild. *You said—Dark?*

Some mourning is capable of going on forever like a crinoline skirt as it grazes the street in bad weather, the tatting damp & oddly rooted, rising up.

It is also winter here & near the last day of a year. The autumn is done with its physician's visit to my body's case, its paradise & remedy.

One day I will be buried with the ashes of my familiars, near my father within a moment of a brook at Slippery Rock. One day I will be the daughter of a tailor & be born into a combed blanket of brindled fleece, lyric running down the honey scarp & bluffs.

Dark? *I washed the Adjective.*

It is not true—what you told me of the starlings—that they will hear tell of the fascicles of tulle & seed. There is no rumor among them.

One day I will return to the North & live here in a bright October that goes on & on, like a flightless cambric morning that will not stop. *Is this— Sir—what you asked me to tell you?*

Bird, Singing—

Haute Couture Vulgarity

16 July

To Recipient Unknown—

I am moved, Sir, by the plangency of the hand as it curls out from between the bars to unchain its palmer's chastity, a mummer's wave to Media, the angst of evening news in the blackened blue horizon of a vulgar supper-time, at the long Holy table of austere woolly feast. There will be ruin in unwelcome worldliness.

Imperial wizards roam the south of things, white Trash Arcana, cleaning this pale earth with their long rayon robes. There is much to be said for shrouding—spells cast in the old fraternal chants, the brotherhood—no one knows the Riff, the tune, but they—who understand the incensed, the insensible, the Song. I have been unwelcome in diurnal worlds. These people immolate themselves for cause, & I am mere effect, no Flame.

In the pageantries of mystics—in the hereafter & the heretofore, the Schutz-staffel pulses like an insect swarm in heat—everything which has power is Rhythmic & plagued. Hail then to the arms & legs which move in unison, to those who sleep or fly by night, the syncopated guard which guards this land from any but the bluest eye.

In Tornado Alley, the storms come like holy bowling balls down a long beige lane, striking the Most Mundane, the Plain, the God-Fearing Simple, the Moonfaced, the Righteous, the Just Married, the Unfashioned, the Accidentally Aryan Kin. This weather—an unwelcome shaman, punk funnel, white magic, black sheep, all through the oat belt, land of a sepia retrouvé charm. *Then why not buy a goddamn big Winnebago —& Drive.*

You should be glad, Sir, after all, not to live near me. I have too much of the martyr, would set myself ablaze—just for the bright light of the fire, a curiosity, for a cause if I had one, a Flame.

Could we see all we hope, or hear the whole we fear told tranquil, like another tale, there would be madness near.

Haute Couture Vulgarity

The church steeple of exact midnight, erect in the unheard of mist of now, too warm to be Real, the cat's low yowling, hellering in fight or Heat, in the mist, my darling, each of us will be taken to a corridor somewhere, one by one & held down by the wrists—Be Good, this will hurt a little, hypodermically. Be pristine in excess Rhetoric, vary the baroque of the High Romantic Tongue, regard the Nun starving for idea. There will be ruin in a new world worldliness.

All are very naughty, & I am naughtiest of all,
Ever—

> *His,*
> *Penitent Friend*

Pompeian

From a bed of lapilli & ash twelve feet or more
Deep, I wake in unreasonably fertile earth from my scorian

Sleep to find the blue Vesuvian
Letter in your own stark hand.

In the hollows left by what you will
Not say—wild & blessed as the Virgilian

Graffiti & obscenities left on my walls in the night, claw marks in
A sleep's oxygeny chamber, House of the Lupine

Brood—I am in your Hand. The wolves have been robbing
The mail, carrying off the incorporeal for their young.

I am chastened by this fact, that always, after
A calamity, there is a rain of predators—

Peculiar as they are, they will outsurvive us all
Like thieves. In the House of the Surgeon, implements will

Come unearthed—primitive as they are, in their case
They form a temple to the body's hollow

Influence, after it is Done. Would this
Too be a form of grovelling?

Evangelical

The Hood is far under way & I think it a Beauty.
You resemble the one who wears

The cloth mask & is paid for putting
Down a man—the gentility of strangers is stranger

Than the sweetness of the more material, a friend.
These behaviors of the year bewilder

Me, the branches do not know
To flourish or to char & bend, like the evangelicals.

I wanted so much to mingle with them
In their pageantry, herding like pachyderms

In their dry domain, standing still, grazing
On nothing, like flocks of firemen asbestos-

Robed, collecting on a parking lot, witnessing
A velvet building as it burns to ground.

Ninety-seven percent of my world is wizardry,
Three percent is organ, bone.

I was a passenger or a witness
In the crowd, anonymous & angelical.

Does not my heart astound you;
An executioner's career is all assent.

Into Those Great Countries
of the Blue Sky of Which We
Don't Know Anything

16 March

Master—

Today has been a fair day, very still & blue. Tonight the snow will hunch on branches, shifting slightly like chicks hatched in a metal drawer bunched in rows, on the way to slaughter, incubating. The oak trees— ruined bare—tower in the sky like stick figures, graceless in wind, as schizo-phrenic children draw themselves as sticks, plugged in. *How I long to see you there at twilight in the door,* your old oak chair pulled up by the win-dow, counting the white hours until Spring.

Sometimes I think I will be broken by your lukewarm Hand. Sometimes the triremes of the redundant Rush row over me, a Sabbath day of ritual, a few sweet hours, groomed as the fields combed over in aisles of alfalfa wheats, burnt down by Winter, ragged as Crows. If I could have your Hands on me, I would wish them on my face, cupped in the head's heart shape, unpunishing.

Then, at morning, the dowager who dwells in the Round House across the road—a sea captain's widowed wife—will pass on like a wren in dust— bearing her into those blue countries of the great sky of which we don't know anything. Not knowing the Sexton's address at sea, on land I will interrogate the bramble of her yard. She has only a sister, no god. Last Fall, when she buried her garden, I watched the hump of Winter cower in the garden path, crouching at the Circumference of her house like bands of Prayers in their pews around an altar lit by blue steam rising up.

What it must be like there in the pitch of Time; in Heaven an hour is for Always, like an ancient Viking tribe in Vessels, rowing home. I will be gliding in the slender dirty canals of the Ephemeral, disheveled as a woman face down in her bed, praying hard for Heat. *Does God take care of those at sea?*

The evenings grow colder now. I miss the gentians' greed, the Hand that tends the gentians' greed. Before the fields go coarse again in Spring, before the fields break open for a wide blue afternoon. When you wake crouching in your small Venetian boat, I will be long sliding toward Oblivion—*you tire me—*

Till Angels fill the Hand that Loaded—
Mine

Toxic Gumbo

Am I to be a patient
Saved by the grave experiment

Of serotonins muscling
Through the old bulbs of the brain, lit

For a brief reprieve of something like a filament
Of bliss for a long light

Hour, then fallen to the hinter
Hills in a squall

Of chemical, the indigenous white
Trash girl, living south of the narcissus

Of industry, where, in a toluene alley
Sugarcane tarnishes overnight, hindering

The bricky cracker soil where still
Some okra grows & other aboriginal things?

In the Attitude Desired for Exhibition

At Lissadell I am the red she
Fox in habitat; Occasion—mortifies.

All afternoon I have prepared my body
For the body of none.

A red fox will be modelled
In the attitude desired for exhibition,

A manikin of faith, a carrion
Of coveting, & vixenlimb.

It was I in the excelsior
A bed of slender curving

Woods & wind, used for curing,
Mounting, & the like—falconress

Motionless
In her gravid nest.

> *The thrushes sing at auburn dusk*
> *Like parlor ornaments wound up,*
>
> *The boy inserting two glass eyes in*
> *His crude nightingale, for torchsong,*
>
> *Armature, for the carry & the carrying on.*
> *You can no more. You can:*

See—how she is
Poised—the right

Front paw aloft, it
Hovers in mid-air,

No gravity
Will interrupt her stance.

Age will
Not treat her kindly.

For the Lustrum

Master, my astronomer—

A swan's song will come only at her epilogue. Luting—the wood, shaped like half a white pear & bent of neck, fretted, the cause of its curdling— she may be beautiful & spit.

Fame should be depicted as covered all over with tongues instead of feathers, & in the figure of a bird. The moon—a lyric nostrum, medieval mute—machina, deus, the secret medicine. *Instructions for the Allegory of the Five Years:*

Before Blindness, Gratitude must be rendered with a consuming motion of the hand toward heaven; paint her with her face ascending, head of a girl with her hair ungathered, loosening light caught there as in the margins of a botanist's book. Show her by a palm branch & a spur of doves, & wounded in the mouth by inclination, abstinence, or red-tipped moss; she will not speak sometimes.

Let her be lean; she is perpetually hungry. Let her hold in her left hand a blue coat that belonged once, implicitly, to Envy. *Give her a leopard's skin.* Drape her thighs in the velvets of India inks, billowing. In the folds, the Star Arranger's lucky countenance should be in part obscured; adorn him in a doublet of black serge. Make a tempest in his palm, mouth of fair astonishment, a copper muzzling. Show him with his face half-milky in her lap.

The weather in the painting should be rushed into the lung of autumn; see that the hues are crushing ones. Of magpies & burlesque & poems, represent these in ten spans. Sentiment will be seen as lynx-eyed, keen; the green exaggerations make her weep. Fear will be seen sitting behind her with a gnarled branch of cypress in his hand. *Pleasure & Pain represent as twins; they are back to back.*

Make certain she bridles, a chalcedony figure, a boy, in her hand. Sundial, shadow of same. From her ear, what has been spoken will be fallen stars composed in silver point. Let the hour be five o'clock, just before the dark gets dark. Still the moment this way, Infinitude. The Years will be seen as Five Moons fluting, radiopaque, colostrum of milk. Broadcast of God out of the sky's machine. Give her a slender neck. See that she looks straight ahead.

Out of the wheeling spikes of the edges of the fields of columbine, the earliest insects rustle in the barbered grass, disturbed by the scent of something new & foreign & formidable. From the shallow diabolic mud of lakes, from the lunatic fringe of the loosening earth, from the Five Years, I will go underground for now. *Show her as reluctant to go on.* Bliss peers near her, an astronomer's lens, luminous body of pupil & sight. Indulge her torso poising there—*Or else my project fails, which was to please.* See that I look straight ahead.

Galileo's finger curls in Florence upright on maroon brocade, the Come Hither hook—tombed in crystal, near the bones of three pleasured popes arranged in three diminutive galaxies. Constellation of white Medicean birds. The river Arno will be muddied green with genius. I will meet you in the monastery, there, near Vallombrosa, in the rain. *Why does this comfort me so?*

Your Lodestar, Your—
Andromeda

Treason

12 November

Dear friend—

In my father's Marl House, all the men die Out, one—in the leather garden, one—in the meadow of the troutless creek, one—in his masked peculiar bed, fast asleep. And my Uncle going, toward his Numidian haunts now—last of the waning patriarchs in my family's line. It seems peculiar—pathetic, diluvian—to me.

Geese like a parliament of petty thieves, heavy in their number, in the formation of a continent of African descent, starving, fierce to travelling—aspire—urgent for Migration. No event of wind breaks the spell of their black-gloved design. Not what they have Done, but what they are to Do, is what detains the sky.

Then your Hand, concaved around my mouth, once a ravening thrill to me—now—Abstains me. The speechless throat is economical, deeper Off, the most dangerous.

My light, which you were endangered by in all these years, puckers, flickers, no event of law breaks the flame. *I deceive for the first time.*

And my Uncle will go deep into his Harvest rooms. The doctors have loped inside his autumnal form, will close him, chasten him like atheists. I admit how curious I am. I Will easily to say aloud what I have Done.

For you, friend, let me remind you of your Treason. *How flippant are the Saved.* Only you & your Flock of fear could have borne me again into this godless chamber of Intensive care. Let me counsel—You—*Doctor as Yourself.* When you become ill in your peculiar bed, in the night's sweat of your dreamless sleeps, by nullifidian Winter, I will come to you from the New World, ministering curiosity, dilating trust, enforcing it.

I had a father once—
And am not—*yours*

Like Murder for Small Hay
in the Underworld

Dear One—

Uncrippled in the kingdom of petition,
I am bent in the shape of the bow

Arcked out toward the particular wound
Of the animal felled. In the tribe,

One kills for game, one feeds the spirit
Of the hunted one, before it passes on.

Sing to her, sing to her.
I did not go to it. I did not bring to her.

I did not nurse the deer on its side.
No maize or small hay, offering.

I did not send her, spirit, on her way.
What was it as I lay aloft face-up,

Awake & let me offer me, to you,
Afloat, aroused, I am afraid

To die, the wildering.
Repetition was my angel then, hovering

At my side like a Beauty growing old.
How simply at the last the Fathom comes.

Not captive, prey, not kill.
Do you know how cold I am?

I was a jealous angel then.
I am a jealous angel, now.

I did not sing to her.

Everybody Has a Heart,
Except Some People

You have fed me on Air too long—a daguerreotype
With its ghostly subtexts of marks & jars—

There—the line crossing the brow
Like Anne Boleyn's clean cotton cap

Soiled on the day of her death. There the odd singe
Of iodine crossing the left hand, wed to mercurial rings

Like spooks—a vapor from another time.
Then—if your pleasure would be so—pleased—

Would you travel toward—me—unpolished & naïve,
Hammocked in a sling of madness as unjarring

As your hand when you wake me carefully
To tell me of the news that I have steeled

Myself against for a thousand mornings
Before this one?

(F O U R)

Moving On in the Dark Like Loaded Boats at Night, Though There Is No Course, There Is Boundlessness

Master, then This—I crossed my father's gate.
Once, I walked into the northern lake

Dazzled by the lubricious feel of old botched
Leaves. When he died, he went on like a loaded

Trout stream—toward a Body larger than this one
Is, wading hip-high in the loaded

Dark of boneless water, moving On.
After Pennsylvania, I couldn't breathe.

Why would what died once keep on dying off
Over & over like a seam in an old velvet coat?

Every night I am the same brilliant fluke
Rising from my bed like a cut-

Throat trout listening for Trick, not
Moving, bound—& if you die of air as Well

The stream will sew itself shut—my lodengreen gills
Will be rouged past Recognition in a vein of metal ore.

When the boat leaves the lake stacked with odd
Amphibians tinned in salt, the metalled lids

Will glint like zippers, marlin,
Stars. In this half-lured life all

Night long I will listen for you, loaded
Like an ark, Boundless, Void

Of course—moving On.
How long how on how oft how long.

Your Cromwell, Your Thomas More

In ruthless October, the salt flats dry out.
Meats will go bad; there will be nothing to Preserve.

Take your Wolsey, your Thomas More, your boys wrapt
In velvet, foxfurs & lynx, cloths embroidered from Far east,

Take them home with you & listen to their taking Heed.
Go in fear of the Body's uncial script, its scheme, its ruthlessness,

Its low river of sleep & wrongful dirge.
Which of us will be Mistaken?

I am detached from the Thames of mine now—look
That I lie Alone in my chamber, Solicitor, profound asleep.

I am chastened, misshapen wings. Or womanly.
Take your Cromwell, your cardinal sins, your Earl,

Your lord & chancellor, your castles marred
By arch & dank distress, your England, your—

Oblivion of rain, the luminous text, your trespasses—
Your bluster, blackmail & your witnesses.

I will meet you in the district of small Rain,
The fog will be lusty over & over again—

The great passioned Wether,
Who—will lead your salty flock astray?

The Four Last Things:
Do not listen to the hangers or rosins or lubricants of rhetoric.

Do not mist your windows over for the sake of untrained birds.
Do not look on Milk Street for our pleasure gone *to heaven*

In our feather beds, like falcon nests or beardless boys.
As for the dread, I warn you the dread is dangerous—

Your Cromwell, Your Thomas More

A man will execute his
Peerage when he dies—

By the Hand
Off Hym whyche I trust shortly shallbe yours—

I Dont Know Who It Is, That Sings, nor Did I, Would I Tell

November

Master—

You say I have Misenveloped & sent you something Else. In the middle of it all, my mind went blank, all the red notes of terror, blinking. Please to tell me—have I unsettled you by this?

I told Ravi that a fear is not a temporal thing, the moment—now, is Now. It is the next which harms him so. *I wonder how long we shall wonder; how early we shall know.*

On the moors, all the russet weeds have grown there—always, they keep on going on. The rainstorm happens helplessly, like typhus, fills the mind's eye like the vacant oil lamps lighting like a lung with ochre liquid when the nighttime comes on, helplessly. Who is to leave here first, hooded in a yellow cape? *Where shall I hide my things?*

Suddenly, I am stammering in the face of Probability. I thought when the sparse trees began descent, that you would come to me. There is the thunder now; it gives the world a rampant tinge.

He has, after all, an ancient soul; he is unbent by Possibility as he walks sturdy in the rain, steady as a metronome's pendulum keeping—Time. No slicker, no hazard, no hood. If I lose him I will be insignificant. *What a privilege it is to be so insignificant.*

Bliss—is unnatural—
Your, L

62

Grimoire

In the tameless night season,
The griefless wind, it is nothing

That I want. A beautiful fever
Took me down. Once, when the ichors

Lit the vein, the world was soothe & good.
I was at homeward in the murmur

Of the twitching hearts,
The old gone gods;

The replicative beautiful
Was looming all night long.

How many druid doctors
I have known & long ago when druidry

Was my first dream, debriding.
And all of the lexicons here at my hand.

And all the spirit-papers taking flame.
An ethery agonal of sooth & rune

And knowing—this—that soon
My little book of incantation

Will be done. It was a magical.
And it is nothing that I want.

Desunt Non Nulla

Then she is leaning, facing north & numberless in pleated light. How the sheets appear as driven by a scurvy wind, the bedclothes end in quivering, the red lead of their folds asail, Northumbrian. Her face is primitive & spare, her neck an ill illumination, unnatural, prolonged—*Are missing not no things.* One morning I woke in the garden, night's lanterns snuffed & hung in alder trees, & was surrounded like an English leopard quartered on a coat of arms, the night gone in the glass eye of its final thirteen hours. Above—a bird, half cut off from the binder of the sky, flies north. At west, a calendar, a corridor, scriptorium.

And took the book & opened it, to this—a flinched life where nature has no place or folio. The adversaria were gold & partially erased; in the margin there, the furnishings of falcons glaired, their jesses & their tiny bells & hectic hoods. The glove is flanged, a color I will never know. He puts on his one right cuff. The rustre of two raptors, fisted, sit on a stone, a blush of iron, wonder, drear. At left, a hound is whistled up, & bounds. Above the sequence are two copper birds, the one in flight, the other perched. The first is prey; flies upward.

And thou not there—a miniature of dread. *Nothing is not not there.*

That Same Vagabond Sweetness

Odd I cannot remember a time
When there was no World. I am

At home, at callow home
Worshipping the train, the Elsewhere's

Metallic sweetness, whistling. A pack
Of blessings lights upon my back.

There art thou happy.
The noise of the world's tracks

Made magical alarms me. *There*
Art thou happy too. And the half-

Blown catweed & the vagrant
Sky & the vacant apoplectic

Bed shiftless in its vacancy, I stop.

Work

Lord, one day you'll find these in a locked box, unlocked
By your daughter, who will roam with you to the fire-

Place & kneel there at another's ashes, scoop
Them out into a sugar bowl to take home with you to spread

Them on your garden floor, fertile enough for pale
Infertile wintertime. Kneel now with me while I am still

Alive & vivid, blessed by a season of high fever, still
Whole at the larynx & can speak these things

Aloud to you. For one season I have swept
A city by a storm. For you, love, my hair is famous

Hair, my hands are clean, large & white enough
For harm. At the throat of November, when the streets

Are waxy as the underbellies of awed swans, besieged
By wet, cremated leaves, an ancient light lights

The season in its ancient repetitions, old song
About the father, the bedeviling, the histories.

Historically, I am insatiable & cannot be beloved hard
Enough. I'm intoxicated, a little whore, lie

Now with me while I am still holy like
This: *I hid me*—as the lice hid all through the spring

Of my hair, divine in their guise, invisible
Cocoons beating white & more or less white,

Their bedeviling, as they hid in their cases
While I slept face down in my hair, white in my bed,

Little lamb, an innocent. I will harm as hard
As I have sealed the ashes in their urn, bold

Work

As a tendon arcked in the lover's hip as she spreads
Her wing—you are impotent, you are wed, I am

Thinking of the humpbacked trunk, full
Of my things, fifty years from now, the terrible

Crystal of what she will find, your precious
One, your lamb. This is my work.

The Last Passenger Pigeon
in the Cincinnati Zoo

An annulment of a species is as keen
As a monocle held up to the sun catching a page

On fire. I would woo you if I could, bend
Back open like a mythic baring

Bird, backed up against a hawthorn
Bough. This is not to be held against me—

This mere yearning & fondness I have
For the Beautiful—even if my labors should be

Unscored by your yellow eye, even if obedience
Should be taken as an anesthesia before imagination

Run amok, or sophistry—Angel, biscuit, nice little piece
Of traffic. Even if my efforts should be misconstrued

I will go on forgiving your
Extinction, your offense, like nobody's

Business, like your cassia carnations blooming helplessly
In April's carrion, in an onion snow when every wild

Thing is extinguished by the dog days of a season
Run amok. Once, the midwestern sky was so thick

With migrations, we blocked the sun, gun
Metal grey, shot down & shipped

To the city in barrelfulls. Our odd
Marriage is the moment of the last night

Of the last day of the last passenger
Pigeon who died out in a dull spring of 1914—

The unreeling last survivor in the Cincinnati Zoo
At the beginning of your century, when you

The Last Passenger Pigeon in the Cincinnati Zoo

Were unfading, beautifully. On that anonymous
Awkward strutting night, wheeling out of a city's silver

Midst, the last bird died out, monogamous & willful,
No survivors—there will be no more

Carriers with their small white billed
Messages. I was willing to wait like that, in the spools

Of decades come undone like button thread unravelling,
An extinctive case of an unwinding

Species folding, classically.

Everything Husk to the Will

I

And twenty-four wild Novembers, two
Times as long as I ever knew

Him, living—my father unlucky
In the little aristocracy

Of Homestead, beside a century
Of other Jews with ruined

Hearts, unblest by happen-
Stance. What is, what happens, what

Will be. Weirds broke him.
November I am all

Cold light, hard in the pure
Refine of wish.

In Yorkshire wind
Is word, tonight is keeper

Of the hoard, all these Angle
Walls, the black stones wedged

Against each other—yeanling
Herd, huddled in their same

White nulled dominion. To a bad
End, all—by weather, bearing, husking,

Lay. Worthless by winter, I am
All husk to my will.

Everything Husk to the Will

I I

And the nights there, Saxon
In their crudity—mistral, guttural,

Ruined by the masterwind. Inclination
Is a little aristocracy. Genetic is

Heroic in conviction, is
The keeper of the wound, a free

Will offering, turned—down.
As for the lay, it is a form

Of expedition, piratical, a pack
Of chalk & squall

& pillagings. I will not be Teutonic
Keeper of that wold, but fast

In the grasp of the delible,
Borzoi lean, wolf

Hound to my will,
My father follow in

The same white broad dominion.
If it darken if a shadow if

Obeisance if it ruin
I would be of doubtful authorship.

The Interrupted Life

about April

My Apparition—Lord,

In a conflagration of cliff-swallows, there is no President. How is it they know where to go, in what mystery of shape, how to catch Fire, who is to fly First? An attar of wind ransacks the city. Even this far inland, the world is powdered by essential vagary & salt.

Letters arrive all day, bearing bad news & Godspeed. Foundering sweetnesses, loons, nymphs chatting, offerings & antidepressants in lightless brown bottles, poesy from all the World, news from Calais—that he is trembling—seasick of the passage from Dover, supplications, the Drawbridge up forever from Illinois, postmarks of Hospital, Nilotic deaths, pockmarks of England where even the Blessed one goes on his knees—being bashful, one looks at the river, one never looks back.

What funnel, what trembling, what absolute Monarchy how—do the swallows know what shape to take, what supposition—their only elegance?

They hurt me;
I grow older.

Everything in the world casts its shadow constantly, constantly, even in the dusk at Istanbul. An apple falls in the night like a sleigh stopped still in snow; a cradle quits rocking. An apple falls in night. The cliff-swallows bank, ascend.

How Can It Be I Am No Longer I

Winter was the ravaging in the scarified
Ghost garden, a freak of letters crossing down a rare

Path bleak with poplars. Only the yew were a crewel
Of kith at the fieldstone wall, annulled

As a dulcimer cinched in a green velvet sack.
To be damaged is to endanger—taut as the stark

Throats of castrati in their choir, lymphless & fawning
& pale. The miraculous conjoining

Where the beamless air harms our self & lung,
Our three-chambered heart & sternum,

Where two made a monstrous
Braid of other, ravishing.

To damage is an animal hunch
& urge, thou fallen—the marvellous much

Is the piece of Pleiades the underworld calls
The nightsky from their mud & rime. Perennials

Ghost the ground & underground the coffled
Veins, an aneurism of the ice & spectacle.

I would not speak again. How flinching
The world will seem—in the lynch

Of light as I sail home in a winter steeled
For the deaths of the few loved left living I will

Always love. I was a flint
To bliss & barbarous, a bristling

Of tracks like a starfish carved on his inner arm,
A tindering of tissue, a reliquary, twinned.

A singe of salt-hay shrouds the orchard-skin,
That I would be—lukewarm, mammalian, even then,

How Can It Be I Am No Longer I

In winter when moss sheathes every thing alive
& everything not or once alive.

That I would be—dryadic, gothic, fanatic against
The vanishing; I will not speak to you again.

The Sleeping Hollow of His Face
Will Be the Straight Pass of Surrendering

One day he wakened from
His Winterstunde of dying,

To the most gold rustling
Of impending end, from

His own head & was,
He said, to be quit

Of reading books & ever
More. A death is portable

Like an abandon,
You can take it anywhere,

A provenance of haemoglobins
& some fate. And from that

Tourneying, that day,
There would be nothing

More to crave & nothing
More to set the heart on,

No cumulus of knowing,
No rubricant of pulse.

Even I know this—
The eventual caesura

Of the hoarding in the sweet
Conservatory of his head.

And then nothing
& then nothing more.

Am Moor

Am lean against.
Am the heavy hour

Hand at urge,
At the verge of one. Am the ice comb of the tonsured

Hair, am the second
Hand, halted, the velvet opera glove. Am slant. Am fen, the injure

Wind at withins,
Stranger where the storm forms a face if the body stands enough

In a weather this
Cripple & this rough. Am shunt. Was moon-shaped helmet left

In bog, was condition
Of a spirit shorn, childlike & herd. Was Andalusian, ambsace,

Bird. Am kept.
Was keeper of the badly marred, was furious done god, was

Patient, was bad
Luck, was nurse. Ninety badly wounded men lay baying

In the reddened reedy
Hay of Saxony, was surgeon to their flinch & hoop, was hospice

To their torso hall,
Was numinous creature to their dying

Off. Am numb.
Was shoulder & queer luck. Am among.

Was gaunt.
Was—why—for the mutton & moss. Was the rented room.

Was chamber & ambage
& tender & burn. Am esurient, was the hungry form.

Am anatomy.
Was the bleating thing.

Notes

In the poems, many of the italicized passages without notation are from *The Letters of Emily Dickinson*. Edited by Thomas H. Johnson. Cambridge: The Belknap Press of Harvard University Press, 1958.

In the following notes, when I indicate a source, it does not necessarily mean that the quotation is verbatim. In the notes, as in the poems, archaic or anomalous spellings are intended. I use the term *refract* to mean—a nod, a pilfering—an homage, in each case, to the Original.

ONE

Carrowmore is a megalithic cemetery outside Sligo, Ireland. Many of the neglected monuments, some dating back to 4000 BC, have been partially destroyed, but three well-preserved dolmens & a rough stone circle still remain. The cremated remains of the land's original inhabitants are buried there, marked by the circumference of the stones.

Also, None Among Us Has Seen God is a line from the poem *Epistle to Be Left in the Earth* by Archibald MacLeish *(New Found Land, 1930)*.

A Rome Beauty is the name of one of the more than 10,000 varieties of chance seedling winter apples. *Heaven paints its wild irregularity* is a line from "November" of *The Shepherd's Calendar* by John Clare.

Unholy draws upon the text *The 36 Dramatic Situations* by Georges Polti, which reduces all possible dramaturgy to thirty-six possible situations. In response to an even more stringent theory which further diminishes all mortal possibilities down to a mere dozen things, I halved again that figure & came up with Six.
The term *Sentimentia,* a State of Being invented by Liam Rector, is that odd cross between dementia & sentimentality.
The final stanzas of the poem are based on the last scene in August Strindberg's *Miss Julie.*

A Brief History of Asylum was, in part, inspired by Jonathan Miller's documentary *On Madness.* Part of this film documents the fates of those incarcerated in one of America's first public asylums in the Commonwealth of Virginia. The film also recounts the history of the practice of lobotomy at the beginning of the twentieth century as a cure for schizophrenia.
The three italicized lines are quoted from the poem *Runagate, Runagate* by Robert E. Hayden.

The Supernatural Is Only the Natural, Disclosed is taken from a letter from Emily Dickinson to Thomas Wentworth Higginson, February 1863.

In **Obsession, Compulsion,** line one is an adaptation from a letter from ED to Higginson, dated 7 June 1862—*My dying Tutor told me that he would like to live till I had been a poet, but Death was much of Mob as I could master—then. . . .*

Notes

When the Gods Go, Half-Gods Arrive is refracted from Emerson's *Give All to Love—Heartily know,/When half-gods go,/The gods arrive.*
At the center of the poem, the italicized couplet is from Izaak Walton's "The Life of John Donne," on Radical Heat, on the act of growing old, on the art and artifice of dying.
A nod also to Otis Redding's *"I've Been Loving You Too Long."*

For nearly a thousand years, at the Tower of London, His Majesty's ravens in **And Wylde for to Hold** have dwelt under Royal protection of a man whose sovereign title is the Ravenmaster.

The body of water in **At the River Unshin's Edge** is a swamp which circles Markree Castle in Coloorey, Ireland.

In **Carnivorous**, the first line of the poem alludes to Anne Bradstreet's confession, upon arrival in her New World, that she was "sitting loose from God."

In **To a Strange Fashion of Forsaking**, stanza one closes with a line spoken by the angel perched atop the city of Berlin at the opening of Wim Wender's 1988 film *Wings of Desire*—"Als ein kind ein kind war fragt er: Warum bin ich ich, und nicht du." Roughly: *When a child was a child himself, he asked himself: Why am I I, and not You?*
At the poem's center, a phrase is quoted from a letter written by Gerard Manley Hopkins to his sister Katie, 25 April 1871. And from Wyatt: *Though I myself be bridled of my mind*—And, at the close: *Schadenfreude*—a lyrical German word for a pleasure in another's woe.
For Kenneth Lincoln.

Did Not Come Back was occasioned by this passage from Viktor Frankl's holocaust memoir *Man's Search for Meaning.* (translated by Ilse Lasch):
... There was a sort of self-selecting process going on the whole time among all of the prisoners. On the average, only those prisoners could keep alive who, after years of trekking from camp to camp, had lost all scruples in their fight for existence. . . . We who have come back, by the aid of many lucky chances or miracles—whatever one may choose to call them—we know: the best of us did not return.

TWO

The title **And You Know That I Know Milord That You Know** is adapted from Michelangelo's sonnet 45, translated by Joseph Tusiani.
The poem is an adaptation of this parable: the proverbial hermit searches in the darkness for the light, while all along carrying a bright lantern in his own right hand. In this instance, I've inverted the image—the monk has been living, unbeknownst to himself, in the light all the while, clasping a lantern of dark.

The October Horse is a figure from an ancient autumnal harvest sacrificial ritual described in James G. Frazer's *The Golden Bough*.
The line *I had a yearning I could tell to none* is a refracted version of these lines from a letter from ED to Higginson, dated 25 April 1862—*I had a terror—since September—*

I could tell to none—and so I sing, as the Boy does by the Burying Ground—because I am afraid—

In **Her Habit**, some lines are adapted from ED's letter to her friend, Mrs. J. G. Holland, November 1865: *I winced at her loss, because I was in the habit of her . . . but to all except anguish, the mind soon adjusts.*

In **Gratitude**, halcion is the name of the benzodiazepine hypnotic agent banned in America in the early 1990's. Like the kingfisher (halcyon-bird), which has the power to calm the wind & sea during the winter solstice while it nested, it had the power to compose.

Dull Weather is homage to the Boys of Autumn, who, each October, *grow suicidally beautiful . . . And gallop terribly against each other's bodies* (James Wright).

The close of the poem alludes to a prediction in "The [Old] Farmer's Almanack, Calculated on a New & Improved Plan, for the Year of Our Lord, 1857" by Robert B. Thomas.

The nobody in **Radiating Naïveté** was occasioned by William Blake's notion of his false god "Nobodaddy."

A **Bodhisattva** is one who forgoes nirvana, remaining earthbound, in order to watch over another.

Have A Seat, Ted is the text of a picket sign seen on a network newsreel, in the orchid hours of dawn, 24 January 1989, outside the Florida State Penitentiary. The occasion was the execution by electric chair of the serial murderer Ted Bundy.

Fair Copy from a Fair World was occasioned, in part, by the work of Primo Levi. And from the work of Thomas James' *Letters to A Stranger* (he used the image more than once): *. . . a ceremony/That wishes to marry an absence.*

His Apprentice makes loose & various reference to Dr. Faustus, first mentioned in a letter dated 20 August 1507. It is known that a certain Georgius Sabellius, calling himself Faust Junin, obtained toward the end of Lent the position of schoolmaster at Kreuznach, Germany. He was soon thereafter dismissed from his position because of his compulsion to punish randomly his young wards.

In **You Can't Always Get What You Want**, the line—*All boys should be nicer* is refracted from Richard Hugo's "The Lady in Kicking Horse Reservoir."

The opening of **Pursuit of Happiness** is taken from a letter from William Blake to John Trusler, 23 August 1799.

THREE

The phrase **A Glooming Peace This Morning with It Brings** is taken from the Prince's speech in the last act, final scene of *Romeo & Juliet*.

One literary case of insatiable craving, retold by the Brothers Grimm, is that of Rapunzel's mother, whose ungovernable desire for **Rampion** (a flowering root vegetable named Rapunzel in German) caused her to relinquish her only daughter in order to sate that urge.

Notes

Haute Couture Vulgarity was inspired by these two articles, first—an omnibus review in the *Washington Post Book World,* Christmas Day 1988, which begins: *Lucie Brock-Broido is the poet laureate of People magazine . . .* & continues: *Nothing inhuman is alien to her . . .* [She] *so overestimates an interest in haute couture vulgarity . . .* The second was a piece in *People* magazine entitled *Turned Off By TV, Soft Music & Sweets, Four Nuns Rebel, Aiming to Keep the Cloister Their Oyster.*
Italics in stanza four are homage to Robert Creeley's *I Know A Man.*

In **Pompeian**, the Master has posted a letter written in his own scrawling hand, difficult to decipher. Before the eruption of Vesuvius in AD 79, the city of Pompeii was divided into nine regions, each with its separate Houses, for example—House of the Labyrinth, House of the Faun, House of the Moralist, House of the Vestals, House of the Surgeon—the last of which yielded an intact & elaborate set of surgical instruments. Excavations have also revealed an abundance, on the many walls of the Houses, of graffiti of every ilk—from lines of Virgil & electioneering notices, to the crudest obscenities.

Evangelical was written after reading an interview with an American Executioner, who earns his living electrically & legally.

The title **Into Those Great Countries of the Blue Sky of Which We Don't Know Anything** is adapted from a letter from ED to her sister Lavinia, late April 1860: *Vinnie—I can't believe it, when your letters come, saying what Aunt Lavinia said "just before she died." Blessed Aunt Lavinia now; all the world goes out, and I see nothing but her room, and angels bearing her into those great countries in the blue sky of which we don't know anything.*

The term **Toxic Gumbo** was coined by Amos Favorite, a retired aluminum plant worker, president of a fledgling environmentalist organization called *Ascension Parish Residents Against Toxic Pollution.* Favorite said, of his corridor in Louisiana, that he & his neighbors were living in a "toxic gumbo" of vinyl chloride, benzene, mercury, chloroform, & other chemicals stewing the air. Here, the gumbos refer to certain antidepressant medications.

In the Attitude Desired for Exhibition is about the art of taxidermy. The slack skin of the animal must be poised & wired in the attitude or pose that the taxidermist deems appropriate for exhibition.
Lissadell, the once stately now decaying home of Sir Henry Gore-Booth, is a classical mansion near Drumcliffe in Ireland.
Also, homage & refract in the poem to G.M. Hopkins' sonnet, *Carrion Comfort.*

In **For the Lustrum**, some of the italics are excerpts from *The Notebooks* of Leonardo da Vinci, from a section called "Allegorical Representations."
A lustrum is the ceremonial purification of the entire population of ancient Rome, after the census every five years.
Or else my project fails, which was to please—is a line spoken by Prospero in the Epilogue of *The Tempest.*

In **Treason**, the close is from a letter from ED to her Norcross cousins—*This is the very weather that I lived with You those amazing years that I had a father.*
For my uncle, Douglas Brock (1924-1991).

Like Murder for Small Hay in the Underworld is my own mis-reading of a handwritten facsimile of Robert Frost's *Tribute to E.A. Robinson*—"I was tried without feeling or sentiment like murder for small pay in the underworld."

In Native American hunting ritual, it is considered necessary, when one slaughters an animal, to feed & to offer water to the carcass so that its spirit can pass on to the next world.

The title **Everybody Has a Heart, Except Some People** is a line spoken by Margo Channing, played by Bette Davis in the 1950 Joseph L. Mankiewicz film, *All About Eve*.

FOUR

The title **Moving On in the Dark Like Loaded Boats at Night, Though There Is No Course, There Is Boundlessness** is from a letter written by ED to Susan Gilbert Dickinson. Line one is, in part, based on ED's letter to Higginson, June 1869. In this letter, written after her third refusal to travel to Boston, Dickinson has invited Higginson to Amherst, explaining that she is Home-bound:

You noticed my dwelling alone—To an Emigrant, Country is idle except it be his own. You speak kindly of seeing me. Could it please your convenience to come so far as Amherst I should be very glad, but I do not cross my Father's ground to any House or town.

Your Cromwell, Your Thomas More makes reference to Henry VIII's monarchical dependence on his inner circle of advisors, his flock, all male. Sir Thomas More, eventually deemed treasonous & heretical by Henry, was beheaded on Tower Hill on 6 July 1535.

The poem closes with the valediction of a letter from Henry to Anne Boleyn, composed during their courtship, & dated September 1528:

No more to yow at thys present, myne own darlyng, for lake off tyme, but that I wolde you were in myne arms or I in yours, for I thynk it long syns I kyst yow. . . . By the hand off hym whyche I trust shortly shallbe yours, Henry R.

The title **I Dont Know Who It Is, That Sings, nor Did I, Would I Tell** is from a letter from ED to her uncle, Joseph A. Sweetser, Amherst, July 1858.

For Ravi Desai.

A **Grimoire** is a manual of black magic used to cast spells, invoke demons, et cetera. Ichor is the ethereal fluid which flows through the veins of the gods.

Desunt Non Nulla is a medieval scribal notation for an imperfect manuscript. When the script broke off unfinished, the scribe would insert this phrase to indicate that *Not no things are missing*, or more literally: "The story has an ending, but I've not got it."

"And thou not there" is adapted from Dickinson's poem *"How sick—to wait—in any place—but thine—*circa 1862.

The title **That Same Vagabond Sweetness** is from an ED Prose Fragment, to an unidentified recipient.

Italics in the poem are lines spoken by Friar Lawrence, in *Romeo & Juliet*.

In **Work**, *I hid me—*is taken from John Clare's *A Vision*.

The term "terrible crystals" is adapted from a letter to Gerard Manley Hopkins, dated

Notes

26 October 1881, from Richard Watson Dixon. Dixon wrote, in response to work sent to him by Hopkins: *I can understand that your present position, seclusion and exercises would give to your writings a rare charm—they have done so in those that I have seen: something that I cannot describe, but know to myself by the inadequate word* terrible pathos—*something of what you call* temper *in poetry: a right temper which goes to the point of the terrible; the terrible crystal.*

The Last Passenger Pigeon in the Cincinnati Zoo is based upon the extinction of the passenger pigeon in North America. After the turn of the nineteenth century, though these birds had formerly numbered in the billions, by the spring of 1914, the last of this species, a female in captivity, expired.
The italics in the poem are from a letter to Richard Woodhouse from John Keats, dated 27 October 1818:
I feel assured I should write from the mere yearning and fondness I have for the Beautiful even if my night's labours should be burnt every morning and no eye ever shine on them.

In **Everything Husk to the Will**, several lines are based on the anonymous early Anglo-Saxon poem, *The Ruin*, translated by Michael Alexander.
The line *If it darken if a shadow* is from the Emily Brontë poem dated 12 July 1836. That poem, written in a child's incantatory voice, tells how the course of a day's hours, its weather—should be taken as prediction of a girl's destiny.
For my first father, David Simon Broido (1924–1968).

In **The Interrupted Life**, the italicized lines are adapted from Ezra Pound's translation of Li-Po/Rihaku's poem *The River-Merchant's Wife*. The title is taken from the name of an exhibition in Soho on the bounty & relentlessness & postures of Deaths.

How Can It Be I Am No Longer I is based, in part, on the deaths of conjoined twins who were connected at the sternum & shared a three-chambered heart—a condition which prevented surgeons from separating them at birth. Though they were not expected to live past even a year, they survived till the age of seven. On the evening of 22 July 1991, they died within the hour of each other.
The title is taken from the opening line of an untitled madrigal by Michelangelo, circa 1511.

The Sleeping Hollow of His Face Will Be the Straight Pass of Surrendering is for my father, Joel Greenwald (1920–1986).

Am Moor was provoked by the work of Georg Trakl. The German title of his poem, *Am Moor,* has been translated as "On the Marshy Pastures," or, more simply, "On the Moors." In August of 1914, Trakl served as a lieutenant-pharmacist in the Austrian army. After the battle of Grodek, he was left in a barn with ninety wounded men in his charge. Suffering great depression from his work, he was assigned, several months thereafter, to a hospital—not as a corpsman, but as a patient. In November, he died of an overdose of his own pharmaceuticals in Krakow, Poland.

—& with gratitude for those who have watched over these—

Frank Bidart, Sophie Cabot Black, Ed Brunner, Timothy Donnelly, Kenneth Lincoln, Stephen McLeod, Liam Rector, Sue Standing, Tree Swenson. And to Helen Vendler. And to Harry Ford.

A NOTE ABOUT THE AUTHOR

Lucie Brock-Broido is the author of two other collections of poetry, *A Hunger* and *Trouble in Mind*. She is Director of Poetry in the School of the Arts at Columbia University. She has been the recipient of awards from the John Simon Guggenheim Foundation, the National Endowment for the Arts, and the American Academy of Arts and Letters. She lives in New York City and Cambridge, Massachusetts.

A NOTE ON THE TYPE

This book was set on the Linotype in Granjon, a type named in compliment to Robert Granjon, a sixteenth century typefounder and printer of great distinction. It is neither a copy of a classic face nor an entirely original creation. The designer, George W. Jones, based his designs on the type used by Claude Garamond (c. 1480–1561) in his beautiful French books and it more closely resembles Garamond's own type than do any of the various modern types that bear his name.

Typesetting by Heritage Printers, Charlotte, North Carolina
Printing and binding by R. R. Donnelley and Sons, Crawfordsville, Indiana
Designed by Harry Ford

Printed in the United States
by Baker & Taylor Publisher Services